"These devotionals do exactly what they say on the tin! They are plain and simple, yet not dull or simplistic. These devotions are biblical and accessible, and I wholeheartedly recommend them to you. They fill a great need in the church for those who would love to know more about the Lord but maybe struggle with heavy reading."
Mez McConnell, Author, *The Least, the Last and the Lost*

"Chris's daily devotions do indeed explore the life of Jesus in a plain and simple format—they are wonderful! For those of us who find reading long, complicated books a challenge, these devotions are perfect. With a consistent structure that simply gets to the heart of the Bible passage, these reflections are laid out in an easy-to-read, clear format. They are truly accessible to all, and I would highly recommend them."
Pippa Cramer, MBE, Pastoral Care and Seniors Minister, Holy Trinity Church, Claygate

"At last, accessibility-sensitive discipleship materials that include all who seek a closer relationship with the Lord. No one should be excluded from spiritual growth or church life."
Dave Deuel, Senior Research Fellow Emeritus, The Joni Eareckson Tada Disability Research Center

"These *Plain and Simple Devotions* are very clear and concise daily Bible studies for people who find reading a challenge. I love the easy-to-read format, which makes the truth of the Bible accessible to everyone. The short Bible readings and simple structure provide a great way to encourage anyone to grow in faith. Chris has a gift for writing simply, and this feels like a valuable resource that will help many on their journey with Jesus."

Tim Wood, CEO, Through the Roof

"*Explore the Life of Jesus* invites readers to explore Jesus' life, ministry, and victory over death. Devotions begin with a context to prepare the reader to dive into an incident in Jesus' life. Readers are encouraged to revisit the passage to notice key details. Questions challenge the reader to think through spiritual concepts and respond to God. Written prayers provide examples of approaching God with respect, praise, and expectation of his answers. Adult literacy ministries would find *Explore the Life of Jesus* an effective way to disciple believers with low reading ability or to introduce the Savior to new readers who have never heard the good news."

Claudean Boatman, Coordinator, SBC National Literacy Missions Partnership

Chris Dalton

Explore the life of

Jesus

✝

Plain & Simple
Devotions

Plain & Simple Devotions: Explore the Life of Jesus
© Chris Dalton, 2025

Published by:
The Good Book Company

thegoodbook.com | thegoodbook.co.uk
thegoodbook.com.au | thegoodbook.co.nz

All Scripture quotations are taken from the Holy Bible, New International Reader's Version®, NIrV® Copyright © 1995, 1996, 1998, 2014 by Biblica, Inc.™ Used by permission of Zondervan. All rights reserved worldwide.

All rights reserved. Except as may be permitted by the Copyright Act, no part of this publication may be reproduced in any form or by any means without prior permission from the publisher.

Chris Dalton has asserted her right under the Copyright, Designs and Patents Act 1988 to be identified as author of this work.

A CIP catalogue record for this book is available from the British Library.

Design by André Parker

ISBN: 9781802543032 | JOB-008019 | Printed in India

Contents

Introduction		7
Day 1	Jesus, Son of God	10
Day 2	Surprising God	12
Day 3	Forgiving God	14
Day 4	Creator God	16
Day 5	Death-defeating God	18
Day 6	All-powerful God	20
Day 7	Suffering God	22
Day 8	Living God	24
Space for my thoughts and prayers		26
Day 9	The angel and Mary	28
Day 10	The angel and Joseph	30
Day 11	The birth of Jesus	32
Day 12	The shepherds	34
Day 13	The wise men	36
Space for my thoughts and prayers		38

Day 14	Who is Jesus?	40
Day 15	Food for the soul	42
Day 16	Light for everyone	44
Day 17	The sheep gate	46
Day 18	Life-giving shepherd	48
Day 19	Life for ever	50
Day 20	The only way	52
Day 21	Joined up	54
Space for my thoughts and prayers		56
Day 22	Advance warning	58
Day 23	Looking for evidence?	60
Day 24	Sinner or sinless?	62
Day 25	A thorny crown	64
Day 26	The cost of forgiveness	66
Day 27	Good Friday	68
Day 28	Really dead	70
Day 29	He has risen	72
Day 30	Jesus goes to glory	74
Space for my thoughts and prayers		76

Introduction

It is good to spend some time looking at the Bible each day,

so that you grow in your faith.

But it is not always easy to do this on your own.

Some people can read but don't like to 🙁

Some people find it hard to finish long books with big words.

Some people find it hard to focus on long sentences.

If any of those feel familiar,

then these notes have been written for you!

Why read this book?

Reading the true story about Jesus can help you

to grow as a Christian. A Christian is someone

who has put their trust in Jesus as God's Son.

We all put things other than God in first place in our lives.

The Bible says that there is a punishment for that.

But Jesus came to this world to die in our place,

so that we can be friends with God—

because that's what God really wants!

A good habit

As we read the Bible, we see what God is really like
and how much He loves us.
So, it's really good to read the Bible every day.
It helps to find a time that suits you, and then stick with it!
Some people like to do this first thing in the morning.
Other people choose to do it in the evening or at bedtime.
Whatever works for you is fine. If you miss a day, don't worry!

All about the Gospels

Gospel means "good news".
In the Bible, the Gospels are true stories of Jesus' life
(biographies).
There are 4 Gospels: Matthew, Mark, Luke and John.
Each Gospel is written for different kinds of readers,
and so they focus on slightly different things.

- Matthew wrote to people with a Jewish background.
  He often included quotes from the Old Testament
  to show how Jesus fulfilled God's promises.

- Mark wrote a short Gospel
  to get down the facts about Jesus.
  It may be the first Gospel that was written down.
  Jesus' friends thought that He might return soon.
  When they saw it wasn't going to be that quick,
  Mark wrote down Jesus' true story for others to read.

- Luke was a Gentile (a non-Jew) and a doctor.
  He wrote so that other Gentiles could be sure
  of the facts about Jesus
  and know that He was the Saviour for all people.

- John wrote much later (we think) and he wanted people
  to understand Jesus and His teaching more deeply.
  John's Gospel includes lots more teaching than the others.
  It has layers—a bit like an onion!

We're going to look at 7 or 8 passages from each Gospel.
We will get a bigger picture of who Jesus is
by seeing His life from different angles.
We'll start with Mark, because it's short and fast-paced
and written in everyday words.
It starts when Jesus is 30 years old.

Day 1 — Jesus, Son of God

Mark 1 verses 1 and 9-11

1 This is the beginning of the good news
about Jesus the Messiah, the Son of God. ...

9 At that time Jesus came from Nazareth in Galilee.
John baptised Jesus in the Jordan river.

10 Jesus was coming up out of the water.
Just then he saw heaven being torn open.
Jesus saw the Holy Spirit coming down on him
like a dove.

11 A voice spoke to him from heaven.
It said, "You are my Son, and I love you.
I am very pleased with you."

More info

God is only one God. He has been God for ever.
He has also always existed as three "Persons":
God the Father, God the Son (Jesus),
and God the Holy Spirit.
God is the God of loving relationship!
Messiah means God's promised King and Saviour.

Some things to notice

Mark wants us to know who Jesus is.

He wants us to know that it's GOOD news that Jesus came.

Jesus is the Son of God the Father. Jesus is God!

The Holy Spirit gave Jesus power for the work He came to do.

As Jesus began his ministry,

God the Father spoke to Him out loud,

to confirm His love for Him.

Some questions to think about

- Why is the Father pleased with Jesus?
- Do I think it helped Jesus to see the Holy Spirit
  and to hear His Father's voice? Why?
- If I am a Christian, God loves and accepts me,
  and I have His Spirit to help me.
  What does this mean to me today?

Some words to pray

Loving Father, thank You that You love me and want to bless me.

Thank You that Jesus is Good News.

Thank You that Jesus came so I could know Your love.

Please help me to be confident today

that You have good plans for me

and that You have good work for me to do for You,

because You love me.

I need help to live for You,

so please fill me with Your Holy Spirit.

I ask these things in Jesus' name,

for my good and for Your glory. Amen.

Day 2 Surprising God

What's going on?

Jesus was in a house in Capernaum.

Many people came to see Him.

Mark 2 verses 3-5

3 Four of those who came were carrying a man
who could not walk.

4 But they could not get him close to Jesus
because of the crowd.
So they made a hole
by digging through the roof above Jesus.
Then they lowered the man through it on a mat.

5 Jesus saw their faith. So he said to the man,
"Son, your sins are forgiven."

Some things to notice

This is a big story. We will look at it some more on Day 3.

The man's friends didn't give up when they couldn't get in.

Their faith in Jesus could be seen by their actions.

They really believed that Jesus could heal their friend!

The man was completely dependent on his friends.

Jesus didn't respond in the way people expected.

More info

At that time, people believed that sickness or having a disability meant that you or your parents had sinned. Even the disciples (Jesus' friends) thought it was true! BUT Jesus said it wasn't true (in John's Gospel, chapter 9). Maybe people had told the sick man that he was a really bad sinner, all his life. He needed to hear that he was forgiven, just as much as he needed to be healed.

Some questions to think about

- When I ask Jesus to help my friends, do I give up too easily?
- How do I feel when God responds in a way I'm not expecting?
- How much do I value God's forgiveness? Does it shape my prayers?

Some words to pray

Loving Father, thank You that I can bring my friends to You in my mind when I pray. Thank You that You want them to know You and Your forgiveness. Help me not to give up talking to them and praying for them. I need help to live for You, so please fill me with Your Spirit. I ask these things in Jesus' name. Amen.

Day 3 Forgiving God

✝ What's going on?

Jesus said that the man's sins were forgiven.

Some people thought that Jesus had said something evil.

Only God can forgive sins.

These people didn't believe that Jesus is God.

In the passage you are about to read, Jesus is speaking.

Mark 2 verses 9-12

9 "Is it easier to say to this man, 'Your sins are forgiven'?

Or to say, 'Get up, take your mat and walk'?

10 But I want you to know that the Son of Man

has authority on earth to forgive sins."

So Jesus spoke to the man who could not walk.

11 "I tell you," he said, "get up.

Take your mat and go home."

12 The man got up and took his mat.

Then he walked away while everyone watched.

All the people were amazed. They praised God

and said, "We have never seen anything like this!"

✝ Some things to notice

It's easy to say words that can't be proved.

How could anyone know for sure

that the man's sins were forgiven?

But Jesus showed that He was God by healing the man.

That meant it must be true that Jesus was able to forgive sins.

If the man had been paralysed for a long time,

his muscles were wasted.

When Jesus said, "Get up", how could the man walk?

Surely he would need some physio first.

So this was a really big miracle! The people were amazed.

✝ Some questions to think about

- Am I amazed at what God can do?
- How does Jesus' authority over sin and sickness encourage me?
- What can I share about how Jesus can change lives? How has He changed me?

✝ Some words to pray

Loving Father, I am amazed at the power of Jesus!

If I trust in who He is and all He has done, I am forgiven.

Thank You!

Please help me never to take these things for granted.

Please keep me full of wonder.

I need help to live for You,

so please fill me with Your Holy Spirit.

I ask these things in Jesus' name,

for my good and for Your glory. Amen.

Day 4 Creator God

✝ What's going on?

Jesus and his disciples were crossing the Sea of Galilee.

After a busy day teaching, Jesus was asleep in the boat.

Then a storm started!

Mark 4 verses 38-41

38 Jesus was in the back, sleeping on a cushion.

The disciples woke him up. They said,

"Teacher! Don't you care if we drown?"

39 He got up and ordered the wind to stop. He said to

the waves, "Quiet! Be still!" Then the wind died down.

And it was completely calm.

40 He said to his disciples, "Why are you so afraid?

Don't you have any faith at all yet?"

41 They were terrified. They asked each other,

"Who is this? Even the wind and the waves obey him!"

✝ Some things to notice

Jesus got tired. Even though he is God, he is 100% human.

Some of the disciples were fishermen.

They were used to the sea.

Even they thought they were going to drown!

They were all frightened and they woke up Jesus.

After a storm, it would normally take hours

for the sea to be calm.

But Jesus stopped it straight away.

The disciples were terrified AFTER the storm stopped!

Only God can stop a storm with a few words.

That must mean Jesus is God!

✝ Some questions to think about

- Who do I think Jesus really is?
- Does His power scare me or comfort me? Or both?
- How can this true story help me today?

✝ Some words to pray

Loving Father, thank You that Jesus came

to show me what You are really like.

Thank You that You are powerful and kind.

Some things worry and scare me.

Help me to talk to You about them.

I need help to live for You,

so please fill me with Your Holy Spirit.

I ask these things in Jesus' name,

for my good and for Your glory. Amen.

Day 5 — Death-defeating God

✝ What's going on?

Jairus was an important man. He came to ask Jesus for help,

because his daughter was dying.

Jesus was on his way to Jairus' home,

but then there was a delay.

Mark 5 verses 35-36 and 41-42

35 While Jesus was still speaking,

some people came from the house of Jairus.

He was the synagogue leader.

"Your daughter is dead," they said.

"Why bother the teacher anymore?"

36 Jesus heard what they were saying. He told the

synagogue leader, "Don't be afraid. Just believe." ...

41 He took her by the hand. Then he said to her,

"Talitha koum!"

This means, "Little girl, I say to you, get up!"

42 The girl was 12 years old.

Right away she stood up and began to walk around.

They were totally amazed at this.

✝ Some things to notice

Faith is trusting Jesus even when all seems hopeless.

Even though Jairus' daughter had died,

he still took Jesus to his house.

Jesus gave life to the dead girl with just 2 words.

Only God can give life to someone simply by speaking.

More info

This story points us to a big truth about Jesus.

Through His death in our place, Jesus has defeated death.

If we trust Him, one day we will live with Him for ever.

Some questions to think about

- If things get worse when I've prayed about them,
  do I give up?
- Do I trust Jesus to do what's best,
  even if it's not what I asked for?
- Am I amazed at what Jesus is doing in my life?

Some words to pray

Loving Father, sometimes I give up praying when life is hard.

Sometimes I doubt that You can help.

I'm sorry for times when my faith in You fails. Please forgive me.

Thank You that You do forgive.

Thank You that You hold onto me, even when I let go of You.

Thank You that nothing is too difficult for You.

I need help to live for You,

so please fill me with Your Holy Spirit.

I ask these things in Jesus' name. Amen.

Day 6   All-powerful God

✝ What's going on?

The disciples were asked to free a boy from an evil spirit.

They couldn't. So, the boy's father was desperate.

He asked Jesus if He could do it.

The spirit threw the boy into a violent fit.

Mark 9 verses 25-27

25 Jesus saw that a crowd was running over

to see what was happening.

Then he ordered the evil spirit to leave the boy.

"You spirit that makes him unable to hear and speak!"

he said. "I command you, come out of him.

Never enter him again."

26 The spirit screamed. It shook the boy wildly.

Then it came out of him.

The boy looked so lifeless that many people said,

"He's dead."

27 But Jesus took him by the hand.

He lifted the boy to his feet, and the boy stood up.

More info

Evil spirits are angels who turned against God.

They follow God's enemy, the devil.

They can hurt people, but they are no match for God.

Some things to notice

The spirit was powerful and evil. Jesus is more powerful!

Jesus is powerful and kind.

He freed the boy and helped him up.

Some questions to think about

- Do I ever feel that evil is winning in this world?
- Do I worry that some things are more powerful than God?
- How will remembering these verses give me hope today?

Some words to pray

Loving Father,

Thank You that nothing is stronger or more powerful than You.

Thank You that Jesus defeated the devil by dying on the cross.

Thank You for giving Your Holy Spirit

to those who believe in Jesus.

Thank You that the Holy Spirit is good and powerful.

Thank You that He can change us and make us more like Jesus.

I need help to live for You,

so please fill me with Your Holy Spirit.

I ask these things in Jesus' name. Amen.

Day 7   Suffering God

✝ What's going on?

The people who were in charge hated Jesus.

They were jealous, so they wanted Him dead.

After a mock trial, Jesus was put on a cross to die.

Mark 15 verses 33 and 37-39

33 At noon, darkness covered the whole land.

It lasted three hours. ...

37 With a loud cry, Jesus took his last breath.

38 The temple curtain was torn in two from top to bottom.

39 A Roman commander was standing there

in front of Jesus. He saw how Jesus died.

Then he said, "This man was surely the Son of God!"

More info

Crucifixion was the worst punishment at that time.

It was a horrible death.

Mark didn't give details about the crucifixion,

because everyone in those days knew

what crucifixions looked like.

✝ Some things to notice

The darkness was supernatural.

It was a sign of God's anger at sin.

All people are sinful, but God never ever sins.

Sin cannot exist in His presence.

That means it's dangerous for us to come near to God

unless our sin has been taken away.

The temple curtain was like a NO ENTRY sign.

It showed that nobody could go near to God.

When Jesus died in our place, He took our sin away.

The curtain was torn to show

that there is now a safe way to come to God.

Jesus' death opened the way to God for all believers.

Some questions to think about

- How does this story show me how serious sin is?
- How amazed am I
  that God the Son has suffered and died for me?
- What is my response to the cross of Jesus?

Some words to pray

Loving Father, I'm sorry for times

when I think sin isn't really so bad.

I'm sorry for times when I've forgotten

how holy and different You are.

I'm sorry for when I forget how much it cost You to save me.

Thank You that You can forgive me,

because Your Son, Jesus, died to save me.

I pray these things in Jesus' name. Amen.

Day 8 — Living God

✝ What's going on?

It was the first Easter day—two days after Jesus died.
Some women went to His tomb to care for His body.

Mark 16 verses 4-6

4 Then they looked up

and saw that the stone had been rolled away.

The stone was very large.

5 They entered the tomb. As they did,

they saw a young man dressed in a white robe.

He was sitting on the right side. They were alarmed.

6 "Don't be alarmed," he said.

"You are looking for Jesus the Nazarene,

who was crucified. But he has risen! He is not here!

See the place where they had put him."

More info

In Matthew's Gospel, we find out that on the same day,

the women also saw Jesus. He was alive!

Other people also saw Him that same day.

2 disciples met Jesus when they were walking to Emmaus.

Jesus also appeared to a group of disciples

and spoke to them.

✚ Some things to notice

The women didn't expect to see Jesus alive.

They were surprised to see that the stone was rolled away.

But earlier, Jesus told His friends

that He would rise from the dead.

He promised that death would not be the end.

He promised that one day,

all believers will be with Him for ever.

Mark began his Gospel

by saying that Jesus is the Son of God.

Jesus proved that by rising from the dead!

✚ Some questions to think about

- Am I surprised that the women went looking for a body?
- How does Jesus' resurrection change everything for me?
- Could I explain to people
  why the resurrection is important?

✚ Some words to pray

Loving Father, thank You that Jesus is alive.

Thank You that lots of people saw Him who didn't expect to.

Thank You that because He is alive,

I know death is not the end.

Jesus, help me to be full of joy

about all that You have done for me.

Help me to want to share the good news with others.

I ask these things in Jesus' name. Amen.

My thoughts and questions

My prayers and answers to prayer

Day 9   The angel and Mary

✝ What's going on?

In the next 5 studies we are going to read about Jesus' birth.

We'll read passages from Luke's Gospel and Matthew's Gospel.

Mary was Jesus' mother. She was visited by an angel, Gabriel.

The angel told Mary that God was with her.

God was going to bless her.

Mary would have a baby, who would be called Jesus.

Luke 1 verses 34-35 and 38

34 "How can this happen?" Mary asked the angel.

"I am a virgin."

35 The angel answered, "The Holy Spirit will come to you.

The power of the Most High God will cover you.

So the holy one that is born

will be called the Son of God." ...

38 "I serve the Lord," Mary answered.

"May it happen to me just as you said it would."

Then the angel left her.

✝ Some things to notice

Mary wanted to know how this was going to happen.

She was engaged to Joseph, but they hadn't slept together.

Mary was a virgin. Virgins cannot have babies!

The angel said that the child would be a gift from God.

The Holy Spirit would supernaturally place Jesus in Mary.

Jesus is the unique Son of God. He is 100% God.

Jesus is holy, because God is holy.

"Holy" means special and sinless.

Because Jesus is holy and never sins, He can save sinners.

✝ Some questions to think about

- How do I think Mary felt?
- If I were Mary, would I say "yes" to God?
- What does it mean to me that Jesus is holy?

✝ Some words to pray

Loving Father, thank You for the awesome gift of Jesus.

Thank You that He is the promised one, Your only Son.

Thank You that Mary said "yes" to You.

Thank You for her servant heart. It's such an amazing true story.

Please help me to understand it more and more.

Please help me to be able to share this truth with others.

I need help to live for You,

so please fill me with Your Holy Spirit.

I ask these things in Jesus' name,

for my good and for Your glory. Amen.

Day 10   The angel and Joseph

Matthew 1 verses 18-21

18 This is how the birth of Jesus the Messiah came about.

His mother Mary and Joseph

had promised to get married.

But before they started to live together,

it became clear that she was going to have a baby.

She became pregnant by the power of the Holy Spirit.

19 Her husband Joseph was faithful to the law.

But he did not want to put her to shame in public.

So he planned to divorce her quietly.

20 But as Joseph was thinking about this,

an angel appeared to him in a dream. The angel said,

"Joseph, son of David, don't be afraid

to take Mary home as your wife.

The baby inside her is from the Holy Spirit.

21 She is going to have a son.

You must give him the name Jesus.

That's because he will save his people from their sins."

More info

At that time, being engaged

was as important as being married.

Joseph knew that he wasn't the father of Mary's baby!

So he thought Mary had been unfaithful.

✚ Some things to notice

Joseph was kind. He could have shamed Mary publicly.

Instead, he intended to divorce her quietly.

The angel told Joseph the same things that Mary was told.

The Holy Spirit had put the baby inside Mary.

The baby's name would be Jesus. Jesus means Saviour.

Jesus is able to save others from their sin because He is sinless.

If Mary and Joseph had made the baby,

he would not have been sinless.

✚ Some questions to think about

- Do I think Mary was worried at this time? Why?
- What do I learn about Joseph in these verses?
- Why is it so important that Jesus wasn't the result of Mary and Joseph sleeping together?

✚ Some words to pray

Loving Father, thank You that Joseph was good and kind.

Thank You for choosing Mary and Joseph to bring up Jesus.

I ask that You would help parents today to be good and kind.

Help them to obey You, just like Mary and Joseph did.

Thank You that Jesus is sinless

and so He can save sinful people.

I need help to live for You,

so please fill me with Your Holy Spirit.

I ask these things in Jesus' name. Amen.

Day 11 The birth of Jesus

✝ What's going on?

Caesar Augustus was the 1st Roman Emperor.

He ordered a census—a list of everyone in the empire.

Everyone had to go to their family's home town to register.

Luke 2 verses 4-7

4   So Joseph went also.

    He went from the town of Nazareth in Galilee to Judea.

    That is where Bethlehem, the town of David, was.

    Joseph went there because he belonged

    to the family line of David.

5   He went there with Mary to be listed.

    Mary was engaged to him. She was expecting a baby.

6   While Joseph and Mary were there,

    the time came for the child to be born.

7   She gave birth to her first baby. It was a boy.

    She wrapped him in large strips of cloth.

    Then she placed him in a manger.

    That's because there was no guest room

    where they could stay.

✝ Some things to notice

About 700 years before Jesus was born,

Micah the prophet said that God's Messiah would be born

in Bethlehem (Micah 5 verse 2).

Mary and Joseph lived in Nazareth.

So, at any other time, Jesus would have been born there.

But because of the census,

Mary and Joseph went to Bethlehem.

Mary gave birth to Jesus—her first-born son.

Jesus was 100% human. He came into the world

as a little baby, completely dependent.

Jesus left all the worship and glory of heaven

to become like one of us and to save us!

✝ Some questions to think about

- What is so amazing about God's promise and His timing?
- Why is it so important that Jesus is 100% human?
- The truth that Jesus is 100% human AND 100% God
  is difficult to understand.
  Could I explain it to someone who doesn't get it?

✝ Some words to pray

Loving Father,

Thank You for keeping Your promises at just the right time.

I'm sorry for times when I doubt You. Please forgive me.

Thank You that because Jesus was 100% human,

he understands the difficulties I face.

Thank You that He came to be my Saviour.

I ask these things in Jesus' name,

for my good and Your glory. Amen.

Day 12   The shepherds

✝ What's going on?

Angels appeared to shepherds in the fields around Bethlehem.

They said they were bringing good news.

They said that God's Saviour King (Messiah) had been born, and the shepherds could find Him lying in a manger.

Luke 2 verses 15-18

15 The angels left and went into heaven.

Then the shepherds said to one another,

"Let's go to Bethlehem.

Let's see this thing that has happened,

which the Lord has told us about."

16 So they hurried off and found Mary and Joseph and the baby. The baby was lying in the manger.

17 After the shepherds had seen him, they told everyone.

They reported what the angel had said about this child.

18 All who heard it were amazed

at what the shepherds said to them.

✝ Some things to notice

At that time, people looked down on shepherds.

But God chose them to hear the good news first!

The shepherds believed the angels' message.

They went to see the baby.

They didn't keep the good news to themselves.

Everyone was amazed.

✝ Some questions to think about

- Are there things I need to find out about Jesus for myself?
- Why is it important that the angels told the shepherds the good news?
- How will I share the good news about Jesus the Saviour?

✝ Some words to pray

Loving Father, thank You that the angels told the shepherds.

Thank You that Jesus is for everyone.

Please help me to learn all I can

about who He is and why He came.

Forgive me for times when

I keep the good news about Jesus to myself.

Please help me not to be afraid of what others may think of me.

I need help to live for You,

so please fill me with Your Holy Spirit.

I ask these things in Jesus' name,

for my good and for Your glory. Amen.

Day 13   The wise men

✝ What's going on?

Some wise men saw a star.

They realised that a new King of the Jews had been born.

They went to King Herod in Jerusalem, but Jesus wasn't there.

Herod called the chief priests and teachers of the law

to find out where the King (the Messiah) would be born.

They said Bethlehem, so the wise men went there.

Now they saw the star again, over the house where Jesus was.

Matthew 2 verses 10-12

10 When they saw the star they were filled with joy.

11 The Wise Men went to the house.

There they saw the child with his mother Mary.

They bowed down and worshipped him.

Then they opened their treasures.

They gave him gold, frankincense and myrrh.

12 But God warned them in a dream

not to go back to Herod.

So they returned to their country on a different road.

More info

The wise men studied the stars.

They possibly came from Arabia or Persia (modern Iran).

Frankincense and myrrh were costly perfumes.

They were often used by kings and priests.

Worship means giving God His worth.

It means giving God respect, love and trust.

Some things to notice

This happened some time after Jesus was born.

He was a child, not a baby.

The wise men were full of joy and worshipped Jesus.

They had travelled far and brought expensive gifts.

God warned them about Herod, who wanted to kill Jesus.

Some questions to think about

- How can I keep looking for Jesus in my life?
- How can I worship Him today?
- What are the best things I can give Him?

Some words to pray

Loving Father, thank You for the example of the wise men.

Please help me to serve You today the best way I can.

Please help me not to look for You in the wrong places.

I'm sorry for times when I give You less than my best.

Please forgive me.

I ask these things in Jesus' name,

for my good and for Your glory. Amen.

My thoughts and questions

My prayers and answers to prayer

Day 14 Who is Jesus?

✝ What's going on?

In the next 8 studies, we are going to look at some things
that Jesus said, in John's Gospel.
In today's passage, Jesus was talking to a crowd of people.
These people were very proud
that they were descended from Abraham.
Earlier Jesus said that He came from God the Father.
In the passage you are about to read, Jesus is speaking.

John 8 verses 56-59

56 "Your father Abraham was filled with joy
at the thought of seeing my day.
He saw it and was glad."

57 "You are not even 50 years old," they said to Jesus.
And you have seen Abraham?"

58 "What I am about to tell you is true," Jesus answered.
"Before Abraham was born, I AM!"

59 When he said this, they picked up stones to kill him.
But Jesus hid himself.
He slipped away from the temple area.

More info

Jesus said "I am" and not "I was". This is not bad grammar!

In the Old Testament, God said that his name was "I AM".

When Jesus used those words about himself,

he was calling himself God.

In these studies, I will use capital letters when Jesus says this.

Some things to notice

Jesus is God. He was around long before Abraham.

He is eternal.

The people didn't believe that Jesus was God.

That's why they wanted to stone Him.

Some questions to think about

- How do these verses help me see who Jesus is?
- Who do I think Jesus is?
- What difference will that make today?

Some words to pray

Loving Father, thank You that Jesus is so amazing.

Thank You that He came into the world

to show us what You are like.

Please help me today to celebrate who Jesus is.

Even when things are hard, please help me to know joy,

because He is with me.

I need help to live for You,

so please fill me with Your Holy Spirit.

I ask these things in Jesus' name. Amen.

Day 15   Food for the soul

✝ What's going on?

Jesus just fed a crowd of 5,000 people with 5 loaves and 2 fish.

The crowd knew about how God fed the people in Moses' time.

God gave them bread from heaven (manna) every day

for 40 years. The miracle that Jesus did was like that.

John 6 verses 32-35

32 Jesus said to them, "What I'm about to tell you is true.

It is not Moses who has given you the bread from heaven.

It is my Father who gives you the true bread

from heaven.

33 The bread of God is the bread

that comes down from heaven.

He gives life to the world."

34 "Sir," they said, "always give us this bread."

35 Then Jesus said, "I AM the bread of life.

Whoever comes to me will never go hungry.

And whoever believes in me will never be thirsty."

✝ Some things to notice

God fed the people in the wilderness,

and Jesus fed the crowds,

but Jesus said that He himself is the real food.

He is the bread of life for anyone who comes to Him.

He will provide for those who trust in Him.

Jesus was talking about eternal life and spiritual food.

More info

Just as solid food helps our bodies grow,

so "feeding" on Jesus helps our spirits to grow.

We "feed" on Jesus when we learn more about Him

and when we grow to trust Him.

Praying, reading the Bible,

and listening to other Christians can help us grow.

Some questions to think about

- Am I hungry for Jesus?
- How often do I eat ordinary food?
  And how often do I feed on Jesus?
- How can I feed more on Jesus?

Some words to pray

Loving Father, thank You for Jesus' words.

I think of bread as a sliced loaf or piece of toast.

Jesus said that He is like bread

and He's the food I really need.

Please help me to keep feeding on Him

so that I can grow to be more like Him.

I ask these things in Jesus' name,

for my good and for Your glory. Amen.

Day 16 Light for everyone

✝ What's going on?

Jesus was continuing His teaching about who He is.

John 8 verse 12

12 Jesus spoke to the people again.

He said, "I AM the light of the world.

Anyone who follows me will never walk in darkness.

They will have that light. They will have life."

More info

The first thing God created, just by speaking, was light (Genesis 1 verse 3).

Light is good. Light is a God thing!

John's Gospel says that Jesus is light and life (John 1 verses 4-5).

In John's Gospel, darkness often represents evil.

✝ Some things to notice

Jesus was teaching the people many things.

He wanted to show them who He is.

We need light to see where we're going.

Light is needed for life. Plants, animals and people need light.

Darkness can be dangerous.

People often say that bad things belong to the "dark side".
But if we follow Jesus, he is like a light in our lives.

✝ Some questions to think about

- When am I tempted by things
  that belong to the darkness?
- How can I follow Jesus more closely today?
- In what areas of my life do I need more light?

✝ Some words to pray

Loving Father,

Thank You for sending Jesus to show us what You are like.

I'm sorry for times when I stumble in darkness

and forget that Jesus promises to light my way.

Please forgive me.

Please help me to walk closely with You today.

Please help me to reflect Your light to others.

I need help to live for You,

so please fill me with Your Holy Spirit.

I ask these things in Jesus' name,

for my good and for Your glory. Amen.

Day 17   The sheep gate

✝ What's going on?

Jesus was continuing His teaching about who He is.

John 10 verses 7 and 9

7   So Jesus said again, "What I'm about to tell you is true.

I AM like a gate for the sheep. ...

9   I'm like a gate.

Anyone who enters through me will be saved.

They will come in and go out.

And they will find plenty of food."

More info

Sheep were kept in pens.

Usually, a sheep pen had one gate to get in.

Sometimes a sheep pen only had a gap in its wall,

instead of a gate.

The shepherd lay across the gap to protect the sheep.

He was the gate!

✝ Some things to notice

Jesus wanted His listeners to pay attention.

He said that His words were really true and important.

Sheep need to go in and out through the gate.

The gate guarantees safe passage in and out of the sheep pen.

The sheep pen is a place of safety, with lots of food.

Jesus was really talking about God's kingdom.

We can enter it through Jesus, the gate.

✝ Some questions to think about

- How is Jesus like a gate?
- If I am God's sheep,

  what does this tell me about how to be with Him?
- How do I feel to be a "sheep" in God's "sheep pen"?

✝ Some words to pray

Loving Father,

I don't know much about sheep and gates for sheep.

Please help me to see the truth

that Jesus is the way to enter Your kingdom.

Please help me to remember that He keeps me safe.

Please help me today to pay attention to You.

Please help me to show others that Jesus is the way to be safe.

I need help to live for You,

so please fill me with Your Holy Spirit.

I ask these things in Jesus' name,

for my good and for Your glory. Amen.

Day 18 Life-giving shepherd

✚ What's going on?

Jesus was continuing His teaching about who He is.

He changed the picture of Himself—

from a gate to a shepherd.

In the passage you are about to read, Jesus is speaking.

John 10 verses 14-15

14 "I AM the good shepherd. I know my sheep,

and my sheep know me.

15 They know me just as the Father knows me

and I know the Father.

And I give my life for the sheep."

More info

People knew all about sheep and shepherds.

And God's word often compared people to sheep.

In the Old Testament, there is a famous psalm about this.

Psalm 23 verse 1 says,

"The LORD is my shepherd.

He gives me everything I need."

✝ Some things to notice

There is more than one kind of shepherd.

Jesus said that He is the GOOD kind!

The mark of a good shepherd is that he puts the sheep first.

If there is danger, the good shepherd will protect the sheep.

Jesus said that He would give His own life

so that His sheep can live.

✝ Some questions to think about

- What do these verses tell me
  about how Jesus thinks of me?
- What did He do to show how much He cares for me?
- How will I respond to this?

✝ Some words to pray

Loving Father, I am so thankful for Jesus.

Thank You that He came and died so that I can live.

Thank You for His death in my place.

It cost You so much to save me.

Please help me never to forget that.

Thank You for loving me and sending Your own Son

to be my Good Shepherd.

I need help to live for You,

so please fill me with Your Holy Spirit.

I ask these things in Jesus' name,

for my good and for Your glory. Amen.

Day 19 Life for ever

✝ What's going on?

Jesus' friend, Lazarus, was ill. Then he died.

Jesus wasn't there.

4 days later, Jesus and His disciples arrived.

Martha, Lazarus' sister, was talking to Jesus.

She thought that Lazarus died because

Jesus wasn't there to save him.

John 11 verses 25-26

25 Jesus said to her, "I AM the resurrection and the life.

Anyone who believes in me will live, even if they die.

26 And whoever lives by believing in me will never die.

Do you believe this?"

✝ Some things to notice

Jesus said that He is the giver of life.

He said that by believing in Him, people can live for ever.

He said that even if believers die, they will keep on living.

Jesus was talking about eternal life.

Eternal life starts now and never ends.

Jesus said that eternal life is

knowing Him and believing in Him.

✝ Some questions to think about

- How do I feel about having eternal life?
- If I believe in Jesus,
  how can that change what I think about death?
- Who do I know that needs to hear about this?

✝ Some words to pray

Loving Father, thank You for these amazing words of Jesus.

Thank You that He came so that I could have eternal life.

Please help me to be confident in this promise.

Sometimes death makes me and others sad and angry.

Please help me to know when to speak

and what to say to people about it.

Please help me to be sensitive and wise.

I need help to live for You,

so please fill me with Your Holy Spirit.

I ask these things in Jesus' name,

for my good and for Your glory. Amen.

Day 20   The only way

✝ What's going on?

Jesus was comforting His disciples.

It was the day before the first Good Friday.

Jesus was soon going to be arrested, put on trial and crucified.

Jesus said that He was going to prepare a place

for his followers, in His Father's house.

In the passage you are about to read, Jesus is speaking.

John 14 verses 4-6

4   "You know the way to the place where I am going."

5   Thomas said to him,

     "Lord, we don't know where you are going.

     So how can we know the way?"

6   Jesus answered,

     "I AM the way and the truth and the life.

     No one comes to the Father except through me."

✝ Some things to notice

Jesus was making big claims.

He claimed to be the only way to the Father.

He said that we can't come to God as our Father

unless we follow Jesus.

Jesus said that He is the truth.

We can only get to know the true God
when Jesus shows Him to us.
Jesus said that He is the life.
We can only have eternal life through trusting in him.

✝ Some questions to think about

- How do I feel about what Jesus said here?
  Am I more sure about who He is, or a bit uncomfortable?
- What do I think about those who don't believe in Jesus
  and have a different faith?
- In what ways does Jesus show me
  what God, the Father, is like?

✝ Some words to pray

Loving Father, thank You
that Jesus shows me what You are like.
Thank You that He can only speak what is true,
because He is the truth.
Help me not to be confused or worried
when people talk about other ways to know You.
Help me not to be ashamed that Jesus makes big claims.
Please help me to follow Jesus,
the Way and the Truth and the Life.
Please help me to be gentle and humble like Jesus.
I ask these things in Jesus' name,
for my good and Your glory. Amen.

Day 21　Joined up

✚ What's going on?

Jesus was talking to 11 disciples.

Judas Iscariot, the 12th disciple, had left.

He was going to betray Jesus to His enemies.

In the passage you are about to read, Jesus is speaking.

John 15 verses 1 and 5

1　"I AM the true vine. My Father is the gardener. ...

5　I am the vine. You are the branches.

　　If you remain joined to me, and I to you,

　　you will bear a lot of fruit.

　　You can't do anything without me."

✚ Some things to notice

Jesus said that he is the vine. His followers are like branches.

If you chop a branch off a vine it will die. It will not bear fruit!

Jesus was warning and promising.

He was warning the disciples that they could not live

or grow or do anything without Him.

We need to stay joined to Jesus.

We do that by talking to Him, asking Him to help us,

and listening to what He says in the Bible.

Jesus said that branches that are cut off from the vine

can't bear fruit.

He meant fruit like love, joy, peace and goodness.

Only believers can bear that kind of fruit,

because they are joined to Jesus.

✝ Some questions to think about

- Do I really believe I can't do anything without Jesus?
- In what ways do I try to live life without Him?
- What could I do today to help me stay close to Jesus?

✝ Some words to pray

Loving Father, I'm sorry for times when

I try to live as if I am in control.

I'm sorry for times when

I think I can do lots of things without Jesus.

Please forgive me for thinking it's all about me.

Thank You that Jesus has done everything needed to save me.

Please help me to depend on Him and stay close to Him.

I need help to live for You,

so please fill me with Your Holy Spirit.

I ask these things in Jesus' name,

for my good and for Your glory. Amen.

My thoughts and questions

My prayers and answers to prayer

Day 22 Advance warning

✝ What's going on?

The remaining studies focus on the story of the first Easter.

We will read passages from Matthew and Luke.

Jesus and the disciples were on their way to Jerusalem.

They were going there to celebrate Passover.

Every year Jews went to the Temple to celebrate this festival.

Matthew 20 verses 17-19

17 Jesus was going up to Jerusalem.

On the way, he took his 12 disciples to one side

to talk to them.

18 "We are going up to Jerusalem," he said.

"The Son of Man will be handed over to the chief priests

and the teachers of the law.

They will sentence him to death.

19 Then they will hand him over to the Gentiles.

The people will make fun of him and whip him.

They will nail him to a cross.

On the third day, he will rise from the dead!"

✝ Some things to notice

This was the 3rd time Jesus had told His disciples these things.

Jesus knew what He was going to face.

Jesus gave exact details of what was going to happen.

Jesus spoke about His death and also about His resurrection.

✝ Some questions to think about

- As Jesus went to Jerusalem, He knew He would die. How do I think he felt about this?
- What does it mean to me that Jesus knows everything?
- What does it mean to me that Jesus chose to die for me?

✝ Some words to pray

Loving Father, thank You so much

that Jesus went to Jerusalem.

Thank You that He didn't dodge suffering and the cross.

Often I don't want to face hard things.

I'd rather run away from them.

Please help me to remember that You are always with me.

Help me to trust You in hard times.

I need help to live for You,

so please fill me with Your Holy Spirit.

I ask these things in Jesus' name,

for my good and for Your glory. Amen.

Day 23   Looking for evidence?

 What's going on?

Judas had betrayed Jesus.
He came to Jesus with a crowd of people
who were carrying clubs and swords. They arrested Jesus.

Matthew 26 verses 57 and 59-60

57 Those who had arrested Jesus took him to Caiaphas,
    the high priest. The teachers of the law and the elders
    had come together there. ...
59 The chief priests and the whole Sanhedrin
    were looking for something to use against Jesus.
    They wanted to put him to death.
60 But they did not find any proof,
    even though many false witnesses came forward.

More info

The Sanhedrin was the high court of the Jews.
It had 71 members.
The Romans ruled, but the Sanhedrin had some power.
But the Sanhedrin could not put someone to death.

✝ Some things to notice

The members of the Sanhedrin

had already made up their minds about Jesus.

They wanted Him dead.

They were looking for evidence against Him.

There was none! Jesus was completely innocent.

✝ Some questions to think about

- How do these verses help me to know Jesus was sinless?
- Why is that so important?
- Have people I know made up their minds wrongly about Jesus? What can I pray for them?

✝ Some words to pray

Loving Father, thank You that Jesus was 100% innocent.

It seems so unjust that people wanted to kill Him.

Please help me to understand more

about why it had to happen.

Please help me to grow in understanding the truth.

I often do wrong things. Please forgive me.

I need help to live for You,

so please fill me with Your Holy Spirit.

I ask these things in Jesus' name,

for my good and for Your glory. Amen.

Day 24   Sinner or sinless?

✝ What's going on?

The chief priests sent Jesus to Pilate, the Roman governor.
Pilate could sentence people to death.

Matthew 27 verses 15-16 and 21-22

15   It was the governor's practice at the Passover Feast
to let one prisoner go free.
The people could choose the one they wanted.

16   At that time they had a well-known prisoner
named Jesus Barabbas. ...

21   "Which of the two do you want me to set free?"
asked the governor.
"Barabbas," they answered.

22   "Then what should I do with Jesus
who is called the Messiah?" Pilate asked.
They all answered, "Crucify him!"

More info

Jesus Barabbas was a rebel and a murderer.
His name means "son of the father".

✝ Some things to notice

Pilate knew that Jesus was innocent and Barabbas was guilty.

Pilate could set one prisoner free. He hoped it could be Jesus.

But the crowds chose Barabbas.

Barabbas deserved to die. Jesus died in his place.

Barabbas is like me and you, because we're all sinners.

Jesus is innocent. He died in our place.

✝ Some questions to think about

- Barabbas knew he was guilty.
  How do I think he felt about being set free?
- How do I feel when I think that Jesus, the sinless Son of God, died in place of Barabbas and me?
- How will I respond?

✝ Some words to pray

Loving Father,

You gave up Your only Son so that I can be forgiven for my sin.

In all the history of the world,

no one else has ever been sinless.

Only Jesus can be the Saviour of all who believe in Him.

Thank You, Jesus, for dying in my place.

I want to thank You and praise You for this amazing gift.

I need help to live for You,

so please fill me with Your Holy Spirit.

I ask these things in Jesus' name,

for my good and for Your glory. Amen.

Day 25   A thorny crown

Matthew 27 verses 27-30

27 The governor's soldiers took Jesus into the palace,
which was called the Praetorium.

All the rest of the soldiers gathered around him.

28 They took off his clothes and put a purple robe on him.

29 Then they twisted thorns together to make a crown.

They placed it on his head.

They put a stick in his right hand.

Then they fell on their knees in front of him
and made fun of him.

"We honour you, king of the Jews!" they said.

30 They spit on him.

They hit him on the head with the stick again and again.

✝ Some things to notice

The soldiers dressed Jesus up like a king.

They didn't believe that He was one. He looked like a failure.

They mocked Him, spat on Him and beat Him.

If only they had known who Jesus was!

Jesus was and is the everlasting King of heaven and earth.

More info

The crown reminds us of another place in the Bible

where thorns were mentioned.

When Adam and Eve sinned, God cursed the ground.

From then on, thorns and thistles grew.

The crown reminds us that sin is the reason

why Jesus went to the cross.

Some questions to think about

- How do I feel about Jesus being treated like this?
- What does it mean to me that my sin was placed on Jesus?
- Does sin really bother me?

Some words to pray

Loving Father, sometimes I think sin isn't so bad.

I'm sorry! Please forgive me.

Please help me to see sin in the same way that You see it.

Please help me not to condemn others and excuse myself.

Thank You that Jesus suffered and died

so that You can forgive

all our sinful thoughts, words and actions.

Please help me to turn away

from everything that is against You.

I need help to live for You,

so please fill me with Your Holy Spirit.

I ask these things in Jesus' name,

for my good and for Your glory. Amen.

Day 26　The cost of forgiveness

Luke 23 verses 32-34

32　Two other men were also led out with Jesus to be killed.

Both of them had broken the law.

33　The soldiers brought them to the place called the Skull.

There they nailed Jesus to the cross.

He hung between the two criminals.

One was on his right and one was on his left.

34　Jesus said, "Father, forgive them.

They don't know what they are doing."

The soldiers divided up his clothes by casting lots.

More info

Crucifixion was the worst punishment at that time.

It was shameful.

The person who was being crucified was naked.

It took a long time to die.

Some things to notice

When Jesus spoke forgiveness,

there were nails in His hands and feet. He was in agony.

He could only breathe if he pressed down on His nailed feet

to lift Himself up.

He asked the Father to forgive the people

who had put His innocent, beloved Son on a cross.

Forgiveness isn't saying that wrong actions don't matter.

Forgiveness is costly.

Some questions to think about

- Do I ever take Jesus' death for granted?
  How does reading these verses help me
  to take it more seriously?
- When do I find forgiving difficult?
- As I think about what it cost Jesus to forgive me,
  will I ask Him to help me forgive others?

Some words to pray

Loving Father, thank You again for Jesus' sacrifice for me.

Thank You that Jesus knows that forgiveness is costly.

I'm so sorry that it was necessary.

Father, sometimes I find it really hard to forgive others.

Please help me to want to forgive them,

not just to do it because You say I should.

Please give me a thankful heart for what You have done for me.

Please set me free from any resentment or bitterness to others.

I need help to live for You,

so please fill me with Your Holy Spirit.

I ask these things in Jesus' name,

for my good and for Your glory. Amen.

Day 27 Good Friday

Luke 23 verses 44-46

44 It was now about noon.

Then darkness covered the whole land

until three o'clock.

45 The sun had stopped shining.

The temple curtain was torn in two.

46 Jesus called out in a loud voice,

"Father, into your hands I commit my life."

After he said this, he took his last breath.

More info

Jesus died during the Passover feast.

Passover always takes place at full moon.

So, it's not possible that this was an eclipse.

The darkness was supernatural.

The darkness was a sign of God's judgment.

The temple curtain was a sign of our separation from God.

It meant that wrongdoers couldn't come

into the presence of the holy God.

When the curtain tore,

it was a sign that sinners can be forgiven.

✚ Some things to notice

No one took Jesus' life from Him.

He's the one who has the power over life and death.

He chose to go to the cross for me and you.

Jesus knew when God's punishment for sin was complete.

He chose the moment of His death.

✚ Some questions to think about

- If I were watching Jesus' death, how would I feel?
- Which of the events in these verses most speaks to me?
- Jesus' death looked like a disaster.
  But why was it really a victory?

✚ Some words to pray

Loving Father, there is so much to see in these verses.

Today, please will You help me to see one thing more clearly?

Thank You that what looked like defeat was actually a triumph.

Thank You that You can bring good out of the worst evil.

Help me to always hope in You.

I need help to live for You,

so please fill me with Your Holy Spirit.

I ask these things in Jesus' name,

for my good and for Your glory. Amen.

Day 28 Really dead

What's going on?

Jesus died at 3pm, after 6 hours on the cross.

He had to be buried quickly before the Sabbath began at 6pm.

A man named Joseph wanted to bury the body.

Luke 23 verses 50-53

50 **A man named Joseph**

was a member of the Jewish Council.

He was a good and honest man.

51 **Joseph had not agreed**

with what the leaders had decided and done.

He was from Arimathea, a town in Judea.

He himself was waiting for God's kingdom.

52 **Joseph went to Pilate and asked for Jesus' body.**

53 **Joseph took it down and wrapped it in linen cloth.**

Then he placed it in a tomb cut in the rock.

No one had ever been buried there.

More info

At that time, when a person touched a dead body,

they became "unclean".

A person who was "unclean"

could not join in the Temple services.

So this was a big thing for Joseph to do.

Some things to notice

Joseph was an important Jewish man.

He stood up for Jesus even when it was hard.

It looked as if Jesus was finished.

But Joseph still valued and believed in Jesus.

He did not hide this.

Some questions to think about

- When do I find it hard to let people know I trust Jesus?
- What does that tell me about myself?
- What do I think is most valuable?

Some words to pray

Loving Father, sometimes I'm scared to stand up for Jesus.

I don't like to be teased or insulted.

Sometimes I care too much about

what other people think of me.

I'm sorry. Please help me to care more about what You think.

I need help to live for You,

so please fill me with Your Holy Spirit.

I ask these things in Jesus' name,

for my good and for Your glory. Amen.

Day 29 He has risen

✝ What's going on?

It was the first Easter Sunday.

Some women wanted to care for Jesus' body.

They went to His tomb.

The stone in front of the tomb had been rolled back.

There was no body in the tomb! An angel was there.

Matthew 28 verses 5-7

5   The angel said to the women, "Don't be afraid.

I know that you are looking for Jesus,

who was crucified.

6   He is not here! He has risen, just as he said he would!

Come and see the place where he was lying.

7   Go quickly! Tell his disciples,

'He has risen from the dead.

He is going ahead of you into Galilee.

There you will see him.'

Now I have told you."

✝ Some things to notice

Earlier, Jesus spoke about rising from the dead.

The angel reminded the women about that.

The angel pointed to the place where Jesus' body had been.

He said that Jesus had risen from the dead!

The angel gave the women a job to do.

He promised that they would see Jesus.

✝ Some questions to think about

- The women were looking for a body.
  How important to me is it that they didn't find one?
- What made them afraid?
- What proves to me that Jesus is alive?

✝ Some words to pray

Loving Father, thank You

that no one has ever found Jesus' body. He is alive!

Thank You that Jesus is stronger than death.

Thank You for the promises Your word gives

to those who believe in Him.

Thank You that when I trust in what He did,

I can live with You for ever in heaven.

I need help to live for You,

so please fill me with Your Holy Spirit.

I ask these things in Jesus' name,

for my good and for Your glory. Amen.

Day 30 Jesus goes to glory

✝ What's going on?

After Easter Sunday, Jesus had shown Himself
to His followers and taught them over 40 days.
He had told his followers to wait until the Holy Spirit came
and then go and tell everyone about Him.
In today's reading, we see Jesus go back to heaven.
We call this the Ascension.

Luke 24 verses 50-53

50 Jesus led his disciples out to the area near Bethany.
Then he lifted up his hands and blessed them.
51 While he was blessing them, he left them.
He was taken up into heaven.
52 Then they worshipped him.
With great joy, they returned to Jerusalem.
53 Every day they went to the temple, praising God.

✝ Some things to notice

Jesus blessed His disciples.
When He left them, they were not sad but joyful.
They were full of joy because Jesus had returned
to His Father and He had promised to come back.
The ascension shows us Jesus' glory and power.
He is the King!

Jesus promised other things to His disciples.

They would only happen after He went back to heaven.

He had promised that He would send them the Holy Spirit,

who would be with them to help them.

The disciples worshipped Jesus, their powerful King,

and praised God every day.

Some questions to think about

- Why is it important that Jesus ascended into heaven?
- How have I been blessed by Jesus, and am I thankful?
- To worship is to give someone their true worth.
  How will I worship God today?

Some words to pray

Loving Father, thank You that Jesus is alive.

He is ruling with You in heaven.

Thank You that one day He will come back.

Please help me to be full of wonder and praise every day.

I want to be able to share this good news

by living and speaking in a way that agrees with the truth.

I need help to live for You,

so please fill me with Your Holy Spirit.

I ask these things in Jesus' name,

for my good and Your glory. Amen.

My thoughts and questions

My prayers and answers to prayer

Now explore the book of Jonah!

30 short chapters to help you find out more about our forgiving God

thegoodbook.com/explorejonah
thegoodbook.co.uk/explorejonah
thegoodbook.com.au/explorejonah

BIBLICAL | RELEVANT | ACCESSIBLE

At The Good Book Company we are dedicated to helping Christians and local churches grow. We believe that God's growth process always starts with hearing clearly what he has said to us through his timeless and flawless word—the Bible.

Ever since we opened our doors in 1991, we have been striving to produce resources that are biblical, relevant, and accessible. By God's grace, we have grown to become an international publisher, encouraging ordinary Christians of every age and stage and every background and denomination to live for Christ day by day and equipping churches to grow in their knowledge of God, their love for one another, and the effectiveness of their outreach.

Call one of our friendly team for a discussion of your needs or visit one of our local websites for more information on the resources and services we provide.

Your friends at The Good Book Company

thegoodbook.com | thegoodbook.co.uk
thegoodbook.com.au | thegoodbook.co.nz